I0816471

HI-TECH JOBS WITHOUT COLLEGE

BE A SYSTEMS ADMINISTRATOR

by Tammy Gagne

BrightPoint Press

San Diego, CA

© 2026 BrightPoint Press
an imprint of ReferencePoint Press, Inc.
Printed in the United States

For more information, contact:
BrightPoint Press
PO Box 27779
San Diego, CA 92198
www.BrightPointPress.com

ALL RIGHTS RESERVED.
No part of this work covered by the copyright hereon may be reproduced or used in any form or by any means—graphic, electronic, or mechanical, including photocopying, recording, taping, web distribution, or information storage retrieval systems—without the written permission of the publisher.

LIBRARY OF CONGRESS CATALOGING-IN-PUBLICATION DATA

Name: Gagne, Tammy, author.
Title: Be a systems administrator / by Tammy Gagne.
Description: San Diego, CA: ReferencePoint Press, 2026 | Series: Hi-tech jobs without college | Includes bibliographical references and index. | Audience: Grades 7–9
Identifiers: ISBN 9781678212681 (hardcover) | ISBN 9781678212698 (eBook)
The complete Library of Congress record is available at www.loc.gov.

CONTENTS

AT A GLANCE

- Almost all companies use computer networks. Systems administrators manage these networks.
- A systems administrator sets up networks, monitors them, and fixes problems as they arise.
- Many systems administrators have degrees in computer science. But a person can find a job in this field without a college degree.
- Training for systems administration may include online programs, in-person classes, or self-guided learning from books and instructional videos.
- Many systems administrators hold certifications that show employers they have the knowledge to work in this field.

- The role of a systems administrator often involves juggling multiple tasks. This can be the most challenging part of the job.
- Systems administration is always changing. This is due to the evolving nature of technology.
- Learning to work with technology, such as artificial intelligence (AI), is key to a systems administrator's future success.

KEEPING IT ALL RUNNING

Thomas Limoncelli has worked for many famous companies. These include AT&T, Bell Labs, and Google. He has worked for many smaller businesses, too. All these companies have computer networks. A network is a group of computers that are connected. This allows them to share resources. They might share printers or files. Limoncelli is a systems administrator, or sysadmin.

Systems administrators figure out the best way to set up computer networks to help companies accomplish their goals.

password=grow(“artificial”, “”);
if (element==grow) {window.location= “land.html”;
else {window.location= “artifical.html”; // open web
<font face="turning, validity" size"-6">
by <a href="register:<form> onClick="range()">
<input type=button value="make organic feature
technological"
</form><t><load align="right">
<type face="letter, format" size"-2">
if (verge == 0) {
tempChart = tmpString.su

He designs computer networks. He also manages them.

Sysadmins set up networks. These include hardware, such as computers and

Sysadmins check all parts of a computer network regularly. This helps them find and fix minor issues before they become big problems.

cables. Printers and servers are hardware, too. A server is a powerful computer that stores content for other computers. These computers can access the data from the server as needed.

Sysadmins also install software, or the programs that a computer runs. Installing software takes many basic steps. But things can go wrong. Then the sysadmin must find the problem and solve it. They must know a lot about computer networks. They also have to be able to do many things at once.

Limoncelli is often interrupted. For example, he may get an emergency call while he is installing an operating system. He must stop what he's doing and solve the problem. He admits that this can be challenging. Doing routine tasks and solving unexpected problems are both key parts of his job. "These two priorities play against each other, and you're stuck in the middle," Limoncelli explains.[1] This is why sysadmins must work well under pressure.

WHAT SYSTEMS ADMINISTRATORS DO

Sysadmins set up computer networks. They may work for large or small companies. Some work for government organizations. Sysadmins must make sure the network runs smoothly. This means testing the network. It also means fixing any problems in the system.

Sysadmins manage network performance. This involves updating software as needed. This includes

Maintaining servers is a key part of a sysadmin's job. A problem with a server can slow down the network or lead to outages.

upgrading security to protect data from **cybercriminals**. Sysadmins also solve technical problems. Sometimes they answer employee questions. Sysadmins help keep operations safe, productive, and connected.

CHAPTER ONE

EXPLORING SYSTEMS ADMINISTRATION

Nearly every business uses a computer network. Many companies have several types of networks. These include backup systems, email servers, and Wi-Fi networks. They also include office printers, security cameras, or cloud storage accounts. Sysadmins manage and fix these networks. When one network goes down, it can affect the company. It can make it hard

Sysadmins make sure servers, operating systems, and software are set up correctly and running as they should be.

Sysadmins manage user passwords. This helps prevent those without access to networks from logging into them.

for people to work. Sometimes, network problems can stop business completely.

One of a sysadmin's key jobs is to update software. They do this regularly. Some updates stop **hackers** from breaking into systems. Other changes fix bugs, or glitches in a computer system. Bugs can make software crash. Updates may add new features to a system. They may also speed up a network. Some updates help software work better with other programs or devices.

Sysadmins also make sure the network is secure. To do this, they install firewalls and antivirus tools. A firewall is hardware or software. It prevents people from accessing data without permission. Antivirus software protects computers from becoming infected with programs designed to harm them. Sysadmins may also manage user accounts. This includes making sure each user has permission to access the system.

Sysadmins back up data, too. This prevents data loss. Backups are usually stored in the cloud. The cloud is a network of servers. People access the cloud through the internet. Sysadmins also help information technology (IT) teams with technical problems. For example, employees may not be able to access their Wi-Fi network. Sysadmins solve this problem. They may check the network settings. Sometimes they may restart equipment. They also fix any other issues they find.

TECH SKILLS

Sysadmins must understand computer operating systems (OS). An OS is the basic software that runs on a computer. It helps other software work with the computer's hardware. This includes software related to network features, such as security settings and firewalls. Sysadmins also

Backing up data regularly allows sysadmins to restore data that may be lost during an outage or hack.

install OSs. They **configure** them as well. Many network issues can be traced to a problem with the OS. Linux, macOS, and Windows are all types of operating systems.

Sysadmins must manage hardware and software. Many problems stem from

Testing software to make sure it works well within the network is one of a sysadmin's many tasks.

a server, printer, or other hardware device. Sysadmins fix these issues. They check cables, ports, and wireless connections.

Sysadmins solve software issues, too. To do this, it may be helpful to know programming languages. These languages allow people to communicate with computers. Computers understand machine language, or code. Sysadmins might use programming languages to tell a computer to do a task. Useful languages for sysadmins include Python and C++.

SOFT SKILLS

Sysadmins also need soft skills. These are personal skills that make it easier to do a job. Working well with others is a soft skill. So is being a good communicator. Sysadmins must explain things in a way users can understand. They need to be able to explain updates to users. The ability to remain calm when problems arise is important, too.

Sysadmins must be able to work well with others in order to solve network issues.

Joanne Yip writes about tech. She says, "Many [people] assume that Sysadmins only need technical skills to do their jobs." But there is a lot more to this career than technical knowledge. Sysadmins must also solve problems. They need good leadership skills, too. Yip explains:

The ability to remain patient and unfazed in the face of the most intense, ridiculous, or frustrating situation is key. Even when it seems everything that can go wrong does go wrong, staying calm when tackling problems can lead to more constructive outcomes.[2]

Sysadmins can build skills in different ways. They may take classes online or in person. Or they may learn on their own by watching videos and reading about the field.

Sysadmins vs. IT Specialists

Sysadmins and IT specialists often have similar knowledge. Both jobs can involve network setup and troubleshooting. But there are key differences between the jobs. IT specialists help people with computer issues. They also help users who are having issues with the network. Sysadmins configure and maintain entire networks. They focus on making sure the network is working.

CHAPTER TWO

TRAINING FOR SYSTEMS ADMINISTRATION

There are many ways to become a sysadmin. Some employers prefer to hire sysadmins who have a college degree. Common degrees include computer science or information systems. But not all companies require a degree. Many will hire people who have job experience. Sometimes these candidates have worked as IT specialists. People who have taken

Some sysadmins start out as IT specialists, which can be a good way to gain network experience.

computer science classes in high school often qualify for these entry-level jobs.

IT specialists help people with common network problems. They are often the first people employees call with computer issues. They might help install new

An IT specialist's job is to help users solve different types of computer issues so they can continue to work.

software. They might connect a new printer. IT specialists also solve problems. They may figure out why a program isn't working correctly.

Sam Larson is a director at OneNeck IT Solutions. He says that experience is important. It can be just as valuable as a degree. Larson states, "On average, in terms of resume strength, I'd say a 2-year degree roughly translates to 2 years of job experience, while a 4-year degree equates to 4 years of job experience."[3]

ONLINE LEARNING

Online programs can be a great place to start. Coursera and Climb Hire are online learning sites. They offer IT classes. Instructors can also answer questions

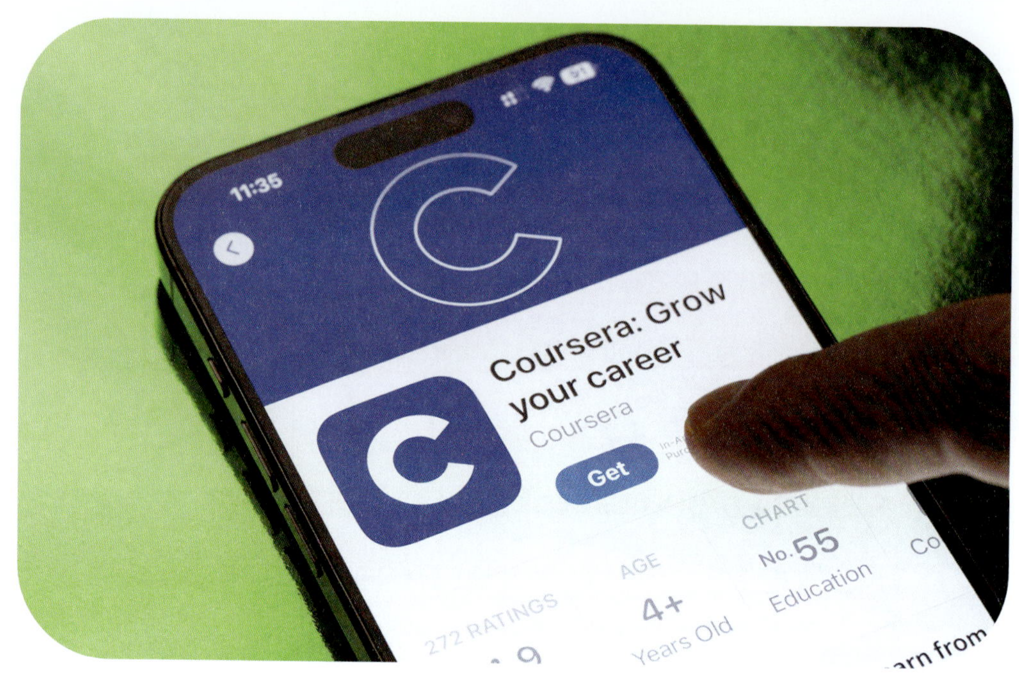

Coursera is one of many online platforms that offers classes in systems administration. Other options include Udemy, Server Academy, and Class Central.

about the tech field. Many people new to IT find this helpful.

Prices of online courses vary. In 2025, many classes cost between $30 and $100. Some programs even help students find jobs in the field. There are online programs for IT and systems administration at many colleges. The classes may meet online or in person.

Online programs can provide foundational knowledge. Students can learn about computer networking. They can also learn about server management and security. Online programs may offer hands-on projects as well. For example, students might learn by setting up a small network at home. This might include connecting a laptop, phone, and printer.

Noncredit College Courses

Students can take classes at many colleges without being enrolled in a degree program. This means they do not earn credits. Taking noncredit courses is one way to learn sysadmin skills. A student might take an advanced network administration class at a local college. They could also take an online class on the Linux OS through Coursera.

In 2024, Skillsoft reported that about 93 percent of IT professionals have earned at least one certification.

Then they test the network. One advantage of online learning is its flexibility. Students must still meet deadlines. But they can work at their own pace. This can be especially helpful for students who have jobs.

CERTIFICATIONS

Some online programs include the cost of certifications. A certification shows that a person has certain skills or knowledge in a field. Classes may be needed to get certified. In 2025, most certifications cost $2,000 or less, including an exam. Students must pass this test to get certified.

Sysadmin certifications can be a smart first step. They can be especially important for those without a degree. Some companies may require specific certifications. A certification can also lead to higher starting pay.

Different certifications are available for sysadmins. The CompTIA A+ certification is a starting point. It shows that a person has the basic skills needed to fix computers.

The CompTIA Server+ certification is another. It shows that a person can install, manage, and troubleshoot servers. Before taking the CompTIA Server+ certification

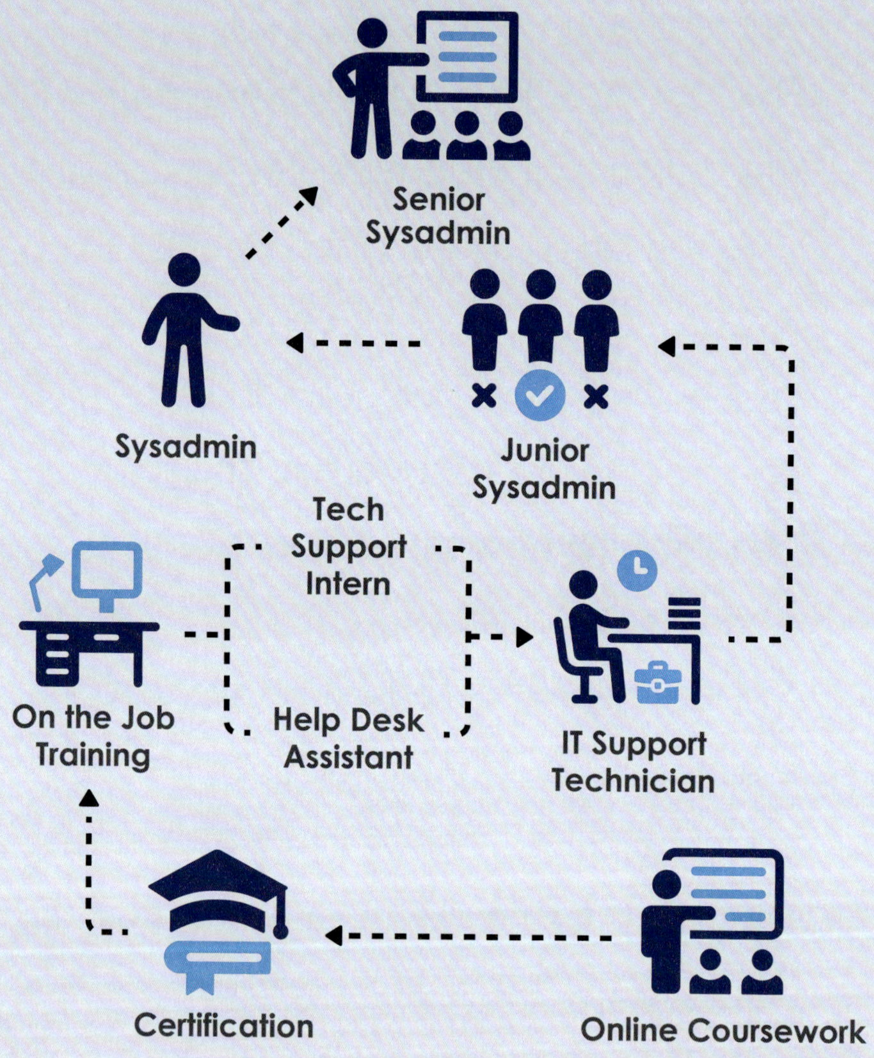

There are many possible pathways to becoming a systems administrator.

exam, a person needs at least 18 months of IT experience. Experience working with servers is also helpful. These skills make it easier to pass the test.

Sysadmins who work with servers need to learn disaster recovery and backup techniques, too. There are several certifications in these areas. They include the Certified Disaster Recovery Engineer (CDRE) certification.

The CompTIA Security+ certification is for those interested in security. Sysadmins who specialize in security protect systems and data. They must know how to prevent attacks. They also learn how to spot threats and attacks when security measures fail. Students taking this exam should have at least 2 years of IT experience with a security focus. They should also consider earning the Network+ certification first.

Certifications are offered in specific computing platforms as well. The Linux Professional Institute LPIC-1 Linux Administrator certification is a popular one. The Microsoft Azure Administrator Associate certification is another. The Azure platform allows people to run operating systems and software in the cloud.

SELF-DRIVEN SKILL BUILDING

Some people prefer to learn on their own. Becoming familiar with Linux is a good option. This is an operating system. There are many versions, or distributions. Distributions include Elementary OS, Ubuntu, and Linux Mint. Other choices

Ubuntu is a Linux distribution for use on desktops, on servers, and with the cloud.

are Zorin OS and Ubuntu Budgie. These distributions can be a starting point for a hands-on approach.

Sysadmins must know the basics of the Linux OS to manage most networks. Current books and articles about Linux can answer common questions. They may include projects students can use to learn the OS as well.

Instructional videos can help people learn about Linux OS, too. Many are posted on online platforms such as YouTube. Industry experts have channels that offer helpful content. Students can also attend conferences or join online communities.

The self-taught approach does have one disadvantage, however. Tonya Brown is a technical product manager. She points out:

Online videos and chat rooms can be great resources for sysadmins who want to learn about a specific topic or skill.

> *I would argue that this option can be the most challenging because it takes being able to manage your time and [being] disciplined. You have to make learning a priority.*[4]

After learning sysadmin skills, a person can apply for jobs. Knowing what the day-to-day work involves is helpful. This busy career can challenge even the most prepared individuals.

CHAPTER THREE

WORKING AS A SYSTEMS ADMINISTRATOR

Sysadmins begin the day by checking their email. This helps them set priorities. Employees usually submit help requests in the form of tickets. Sysadmins get an email when tickets are submitted. Sysadmins might solve the most urgent problems first. One example is a Wi-Fi outage. This prevents employees from working. It must be fixed quickly.

Many sysadmins begin their days by checking emails and prioritizing tasks.

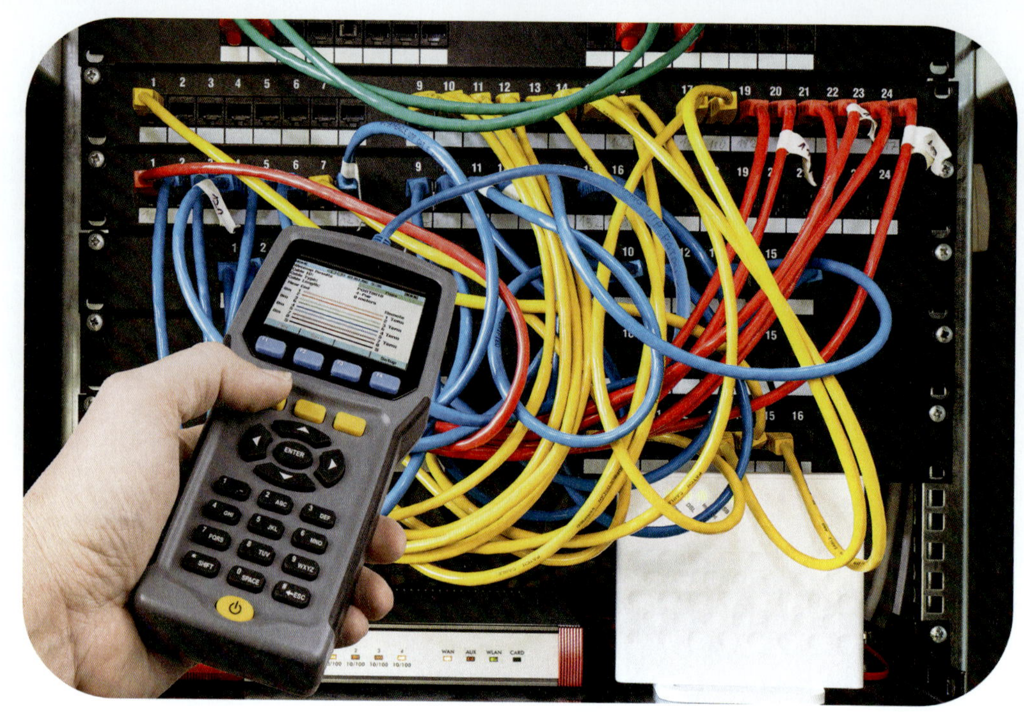

Devices such as handheld cable testers help sysadmins monitor different parts of a network.

Then they tackle other issues. They might solve the simple problems first. This allows them to do the more complex task without interruption. One example might be fixing a program that keeps crashing.

Next, the sysadmin might perform routine tasks. These could include running network tests. They may make phone calls. The sysadmin might need to order new software or parts for a repair. In the afternoon, they may work on computers that are running slowly.

A sysadmin's work is never finished. Networks need to be updated often. New software must be installed. And sysadmins must always monitor the network. Checking the network regularly is important. This is the best way to catch a small problem before it becomes bigger.

AFTER HOURS

Unexpected issues can also pop up after work hours. Sysadmins might get alerts about viruses that have infected a network. A quick response limits the amount of damage to the company's computer systems or data. Solving the problem

Sometimes, sysadmins may need to work evenings or weekends to perform network updates or resolve critical issues.

before employees return to work is key. This reduces the amount of work time lost.

Some companies even hire an overnight sysadmin. For businesses without a 24-hour team, the days can be long. A big network problem means coming in early or staying late. Sysadmin Jerremy Windeyer shares,

"Some days I get to sleep in a bit and other days I'm woken up by an early phone call asking for support. Every now and then, I work a **graveyard shift**."[5]

WHERE SYSTEMS ADMINISTRATORS WORK

Sysadmins work in all types of organizations. They work in banking, e-commerce, and government. They also work in health care and schools. The larger the organization, the more important it can be to have a sysadmin. Small businesses may need a sysadmin, too.

Many sysadmins work in a company office. For some tasks, they must access computer hardware. A sysadmin may spend a lot of time in the data center.

Some tasks, including replacing failed hard drives or inspecting cable connections, require sysadmins to be in the server room.

This is the room where computer servers are kept. But much of the work can be done remotely. A sysadmin can log into a company's virtual private network (VPN) from other locations. Companies may allow sysadmins to work offsite one or more days per week. Employees can often choose what works best for them.

Systems administrator David Both worked at a company that allowed him to be offsite. He recalls:

> *The hours were so flexible that some of us did not come into the office until noon or even 3:00 p.m. while others came in early and left early. . . . So long as one's work was finished on time and we showed up at team meetings in person, we were pretty much free to come and go at will.*[6]

Some sysadmins freelance. This means they sign a contract. They agree to perform sysadmin duties for a set amount of time. Like full-time sysadmins, freelancers may need to go to an office at times. But they usually work remotely. Sysadmins can even work while traveling.

THE TOOLS OF SYSTEMS ADMINISTRATION

A sysadmin uses many types of tools. Among the most important are configuration management tools. These are like remote controls for computer networks. Sysadmins use these tools to perform tasks. The tools allow sysadmins to install software on many computers at once.

The Flexibility of Freelancing

Freelancers may work for one company. They can also work for several different companies. A freelancer may perform different tasks for each client. Freelancing offers more flexibility than full-time work. For some tasks, workers can set their own hours. These include installing software updates or creating disaster recovery plans.

Different tools are used depending on the OS. Tools can vary because of the mix of platforms in a network, too. Ansible is one management tool. It works with Linux and macOS. Puppet is another tool. It works with Windows. Sysadmins may prefer one tool over another.

Network management tools are a key part of a sysadmin's toolbox. They help monitor networks and find problems. Wireshark is one example. It lets sysadmins watch data on a network. It works like a traffic camera watches the road. Sysadmins use data Wireshark gathers. It helps them **diagnose** network issues. For example, websites may be loading very slowly around noon each day. A sysadmin might use Wireshark to find out why. They could

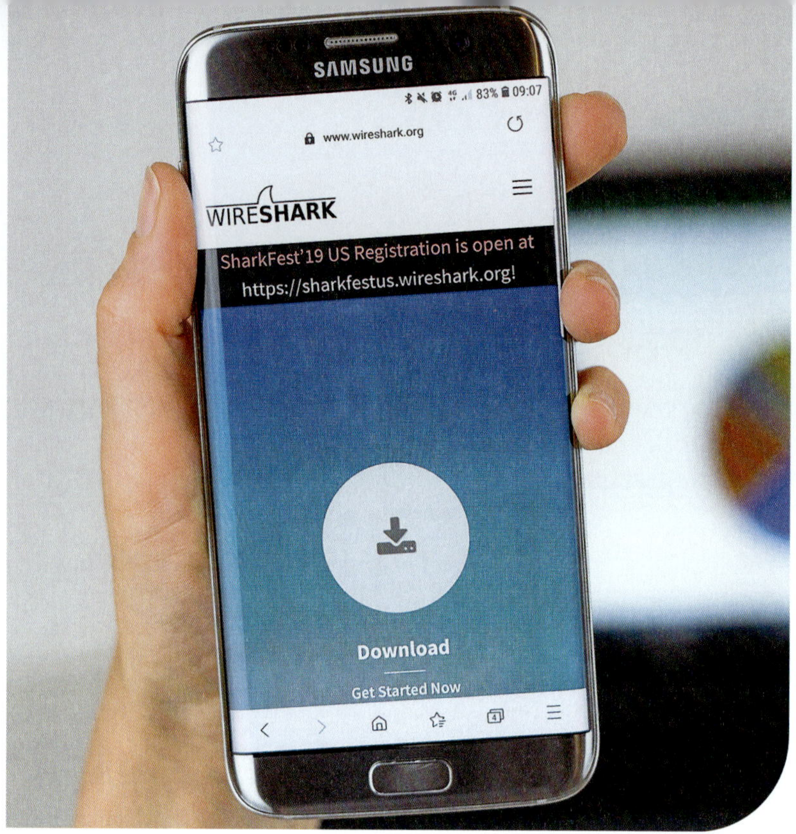

Wireshark is a network monitoring tool that runs on Windows, Linux, macOS, and many other platforms. It allows sysadmins to see exactly what is happening on their network at any given time.

discover that employees are streaming videos on company Wi-Fi during lunch. This may slow down the network for other users.

Sysadmins use backup and security tools as well. These protect companies during computer failures or **cyberattacks**. The tools prevent a loss of data.

Clonezilla is an open-source tool. This means it is available for free. It backs up network data by making copies of computer drives. It stores the copies in another location.

Metasploit is a security testing tool. It helps sysadmins find a network's weak security points. This can stop hackers from getting into a network. Using the best tools is important. They help sysadmins manage their networks. This leads to fewer network problems.

CHAPTER FOUR

LOOKING AHEAD

Sysadmins must keep up with the latest technologies. Technology is always advancing. This means the role of a sysadmin is always changing, too. Tasks that humans once did are now done by computers. Many sysadmin tasks will likely be taken over by computers in the future. This presents challenges for sysadmins. But it also provides opportunities.

Sysadmins must closely follow technological advances in their field, including those in cloud computing. These advances will change the work they do.

As AI takes over tasks such as routine updates to computer software, sysadmins will still need to maintain hardware.

The US Bureau of Labor Statistics reports on jobs. In 2023, it predicted a 3 percent decline in jobs for sysadmins by 2033. But it also expected 16,400 sysadmin jobs to be available each year. This is because some sysadmins will leave the field. Some may change careers. Other sysadmins will retire.

Some sysadmins worry that artificial intelligence (AI) could take over their jobs. Sysadmin Ken Hess isn't concerned. He thinks there will always be jobs in technology. He states:

Software breaks. Hardware breaks. You need someone to fix those things. That someone is a [sysadmin]. As long as we have things that break, we will need [sysadmins]. . . . These magical devices in our hands are so far advanced, yet there are mobile phone repair shops in every city, and they're all very busy.[7]

CHANGING RESPONSIBILITIES

For a long time, sysadmins oversaw many parts of a network. But today they are

Sysadmins must work together to create effective security measures against data breaches, which increased dramatically from 2005 to 2025.

handling fewer basic administrative tasks. This includes installing OSs and setting up networks. These tasks are often automated. Or they are handled by cloud providers.

This frees up sysadmins for more complex tasks such as analyzing system logs. These are digital records. They track what happens inside computer systems.

By reading these logs, sysadmins might discover a problem such as **malware**.

More businesses are using new technology. This has created a growing need for sysadmins. Many specialize in one particular area. Cloud computing is an example. It is growing a lot. This means companies will need more sysadmins who know the cloud well. They need people who understand its structure, security, and tools.

Cybersecurity is also growing. More and more information is being stored digitally. Thieves are always looking for ways to steal data. Sysadmins must stay a step ahead of cybercriminals. Sysadmins who know cybersecurity will continue to be in demand.

Some data needs to be kept secure. The government and companies in the financial industry are among the employers who keep data on their own servers. They often avoid using the cloud. This keeps their data as safe as possible. Sysadmins will remain in demand in these settings. But the tools they use will become more complex. Benjamin Maggi is a tech expert.

Adapting Is Key

Resisting change is often a good way to get left behind when it comes to technology. This is especially true for people in the sysadmin field. Sysadmins must be willing to learn all they can about useful AI tools. This approach may improve security, speed, and creativity. AI may free up human workers from many time-consuming tasks.

He explains, "Looking forward, the sysadmin role is far from **obsolete**. Instead, it continues to adapt."[8]

WORKING WITH AI

AI will affect the future for sysadmins. But it will likely make their jobs easier. When the calculator was invented, accountants were still needed. This new tool simply made their work easier. Likewise, sysadmins will use AI for their routine tasks.

The use of AI changes a sysadmin's responsibilities. For example, they need to decide where and when AI will be used. They must also manage AI-powered software. They must make sure these programs are protected from cyberattacks as well.

AI has come a long way. But it is still developing. Sometimes, AI makes mistakes. Humans are needed to fix these problems.

People are also much better than AI at doing certain tasks. AI can handle repetitive tasks. These include backing up data or updating software.

AI frees up sysadmins for doing the more creative parts of the job. This might be finding ways to improve systems. Or it could mean looking for solutions to common problems. These include weak spots in security and issues that slow computers. Some sysadmins compare using AI to having a smart assistant. AI is not a replacement for human workers.

Being a sysadmin can be challenging. It requires problem solving. Sysadmins must

Going forward, companies will need sysadmins who stay up to date on AI developments and learn to work with the technology.

be strong leaders, too. But the job is also rewarding. Those with strong math and computer skills can be effective sysadmins. This career does not require a degree. Employers are looking for sysadmins with the skills and experience to get the job done.

GLOSSARY

configure

to set up computer hardware and software to perform certain tasks

cyberattacks

attempts to break into computer networks

cybercriminals

people who use computers to steal data or cause harm

cybersecurity

efforts to protect computer networks from cyberattacks

diagnose

to identify a problem

graveyard shift

a work schedule that takes place overnight

hackers

people who break into computer systems

malware

software designed to damage or disrupt a computer system

obsolete

outdated to the point of no longer being useful

SOURCE NOTES

INTRODUCTION: KEEPING IT ALL RUNNING

1. Thomas A. Limoncelli, *Time Management for System Administrators*. O'Reilly, 2006, p. 3.

CHAPTER ONE: EXPLORING SYSTEMS ADMINISTRATION

2. Joanne Yip, "12 IT Skills Every Sysadmin Should Have on Their Resume in 2024," *Smart Deploy*, March 18, 2024. https://smartdeploy.com.

CHAPTER TWO: TRAINING FOR SYSTEMS ADMINISTRATION

3. Yip, "12 IT Skills Every Sysadmin Should Have."

4. Tonya Brown, "Learn the Technical Ropes and Become a Sysadmin," *Red Hat*, August 1, 2019. https://redhat.com.

CHAPTER THREE: WORKING AS A SYSTEMS ADMINISTRATOR

5. Quoted in "A Day in the Life of an IT Systems Administrator," *180 Engineering*, October 24, 2022. https://180engineering.com.

6. David Both, "How Remote Work Can Work for Sysadmins," *Red Hat*, May 22, 2019. https://redhat.com.

CHAPTER FOUR: LOOKING AHEAD

7. Ken Hess, "Sysadmin Careers: Is Your Sysadmin Job Going Away?" *Red Hat*, June 11, 2020. https://redhat.com.

8. Benjamin Maggi, "Where Are all the SysAdmins? Examining the Role Evolution over the Past Decade," *LinkedIn*, March 4, 2025. https://linkedin.com.

FOR FURTHER RESEARCH

BOOKS

Sue Bradford Edwards, *Be a Data Center Technician.* BrightPoint Press, 2026.

Cynthia Kennedy Henzel, *Be a Cybersecurity Specialist.* BrightPoint Press, 2025.

Claire Quigley, *Simply Artificial Intelligence.* DK, 2023.

INTERNET SOURCES

Phil Lombardi, "What Does a Systems Administrator Do?" *Indeed*, March 3, 2025. www.indeed.com.

"Network and Computer Systems Administrators," *US Bureau of Labor Statistics*, n.d. www.bls.gov.

"Your Next Move: Systems Administrator," *CompTIA*, January 3, 2025. www.comptia.org.

WEBSITES

League of Professional System Administrators (LOPSA)

https://lopsa.org

The League of Professional System Administrators website offers events and resources to help sysadmins learn and advance in their careers.

Linux Professional Institute (LPI)

www.lpi.org

The Linux Professional Institute offers information about Linux training and certifications. Those who earn professional certification can also find ways to get involved in the Linux community.

SysAdmin, Audit, Network, and Security (SANS) Institute

www.sans.org

SANS Institute provides a certification pathway for becoming a systems administrator. The site also lists the skills and qualifications needed to succeed in this career.

INDEX

IMAGE CREDITS

Cover: © Gorodenkoff/Shutterstock Images
5: © Journey Studio7/Shutterstock Images
7: © vectorfusionart/Shutterstock Images
8: © Fractal Pictures/Shutterstock Images
11: © baranozdemir/iStockphoto
13: © shironosov/iStockphoto
14: © Tapati Rinchumrus/Shutterstock Images
17: © Yanawut.S/Shutterstock Images
18: © dotshock/Shutterstock Images
20: © DC Studio/Shutterstock Images
23: © Bojan Milinkov/Shutterstock Images
24: © andresr/iStockphoto
26: © PixieMe/Shutterstock Images
28: © Father-Studio/Shutterstock Images
30 (On the Job Training, Certification, Online Coursework): © Nataliia/iStockphoto
30 (Senior SysAdmin, SysAdmin, Junior SysAdmin, IT Support Tech):
© The Studio/Shutterstock Images
33: © Daniel Constante/Shutterstock Images
35: © Ground Picture/Shutterstock Images
37: © Gorodenkoff/Shutterstock Images
38: © KPixMining/Shutterstock Images
40: © Gorodenkoff/Shutterstock Images
42: © Gorodenkoff/Shutterstock Images
46: © VideoBCN/Shutterstock Images
49: © Andrey_Popov/Shutterstock Images
50: © sturti/iStockphoto
52: © puhhha/Shutterstock Images
57: © Wanan Yossingkum/iStockphoto

ABOUT THE AUTHOR

Tammy Gagne is an author and editor with a passion for educational nonfiction. She has written hundreds of books for both adults and young people. Residing in the beautiful state of Maine, she enjoys life with her husband, their son, and two rescue dogs. When not writing or editing, she is often brainstorming her next project. Some of her recent titles are about America's ethnic diversity and the physics that make flight possible. She hopes they inspire and educate readers of all ages.